THE PRINCIPLES OF DEMOCRACY

WHAT ARE MINORITY RIGHTS?

JOSHUA TURNER

New York

Published in 2020 by The Rosen Publishing Group, Inc.
29 East 21st Street, New York, NY 10010

Copyright © 2020 by The Rosen Publishing Group, Inc.

All rights reserved. No part of this book may be reproduced in any form without permission in writing from the publisher, except by a reviewer.

First Edition

Editor: Melissa Raé Shofner
Book Design: Reann Nye

Photo Credits: Seriest art Bplanet/Shutterstock.com; cover Zurijeta/Shutterstock.com; p. 5 Drew Angerer/Getty Images News/Getty Images; p. 7 spyarm/Shutterstock.com; p. 9 Bettmann/Getty Images; p. 11 Hill Street Studios/Blend Images/Getty Images; p. 13 jabejon/E+/Getty Images; p. 15 Drop of Light/Shutterstock.com; p. 17 JEWEL SAMAD/AFP/Getty Images; p. 19 Paul Marotta/Getty Images Entertainment/Getty Images; p. 21 David McNew/Getty Images News/Getty Images; p. 22 Image Source/DigitalVision/Getty Images.

Cataloging-in-Publication Data

Names: Turner, Joshua.
Title: What are minority rights? / Joshua Turner.
Description: New York : PowerKids Press, 2020. | Series: The principles of democracy | Includes glossary and index.
Identifiers: ISBN 9781538342602 (pbk.) | ISBN 9781538342626 (library bound) | ISBN 9781538342619 (6 pack)
Subjects: LCSH: Minorities–Civil rights–Juvenile literature. | Human rights–Juvenile literature.
Classification: LCC JC312.T87 2019 | DDC 305.8-dc23

Manufactured in the United States of America

CPSIA Compliance Information: Batch #CSPK19: For Further Information contact Rosen Publishing, New York, New York at 1-800-237-9932

CONTENTS

★★★★★★★★★★

PUT YOURSELF
   IN ANOTHER'S SHOES 4
WHO ARE MINORITIES? 6
WHAT IS A RIGHT? 8
LIVING IN A DEMOCRACY 10
MINORITY PROTECTION 12
LAWMAKING IN A DEMOCRACY 14
WHAT IS FAIR FOR
   MINORITIES TO EXPECT? 16
WHY ARE MINORITY
   RIGHTS IMPORTANT? 18
WHAT SOCIETY IS BEST? 20
MINORITY RIGHTS............... 22
GLOSSARY 23
INDEX 24
WEBSITES 24

PUT YOURSELF IN ANOTHER'S SHOES

One of the most important things a person can do in a democracy is to try to understand other people's points of view. This isn't always easy. However, it's necessary if a society wants to make decisions that are fair for everyone.

This is especially true when thinking about minorities. Before we can decide what laws are best, we must understand how they will affect everyone in society. For a democracy to be successful, the rights of minorities must be respected.

"How would I like this decision if I were someone else?" People in a democracy should stop and ask themselves this question when making decisions about important issues.

WHO ARE MINORITIES?

Minorities are groups of people in a society that are smaller than the largest group, or majority. Social standing also plays a part in whether someone is in a minority group. People in minority groups sometimes have different concerns than people in the majority.

There are often many different minority groups in a country. These groups may be based on **ethnicity**, religion, race, **gender**, or politics. People can belong to several minority groups at the same time.

THE SPIRIT OF DEMOCRACY

The Pilgrims were some of the first Europeans to settle in North America. In England, they were a minority because of their religious beliefs. They traveled to Massachusetts Colony in hopes of making a better life for themselves.

The Statue of Liberty represents, or stands for, how the United States was willing to accept minority groups from around the world, no matter their social or **economic** class.

7

WHAT IS A RIGHT?

The citizens of a democracy have certain rights. Rights are conditions that can't be limited or taken away by other people or the government. In the United States, citizens have many rights, such as freedom of speech and the right to vote.

If one citizen tries to limit or take away another citizen's rights, the government is allowed to **punish** him or her. Rights come with **responsibilities** such as paying taxes and not breaking the rules.

Sometimes rights must be fought for. In the late nineteenth century, women in the United States fought peacefully for their right to vote, which they won in 1920.

9

LIVING IN A DEMOCRACY

The United States has a representative democracy. In a representative democracy, citizens vote for people who will **represent** them in the government. This means every person gets a say, even if they belong to a minority group.

If every person gets a say, it would make sense for the voice of the majority to be heard over those in minority groups, which would swing laws in favor of the majority. How do we protect, or keep safe, those people who are part of the minority?

THE SPIRIT OF DEMOCRACY

Democracy began in ancient Greece thousands of years ago. It's been shown to be the best system of government when it comes to protecting minority rights.

One of the key features of democracy is the ability for citizens to change government practices—and the majority—through voting.

11

MINORITY PROTECTION

Rules are put into place that make sure minorities are not unfairly **targeted** or **discriminated** against. This means even if the majority wants something that hurts minorities, the government won't be able to do it.

Think about it this way: If your teacher knows there's a vegetarian in your class, she may give you the option of many different pizzas, but she won't let you vote for only pepperoni. This is because she's protecting the rights of the vegetarian minority.

> Protection of minority rights is important for every person in any society. Remember, even if you are in the majority today, you might be in the minority tomorrow.

LAWMAKING IN A DEMOCRACY

In the United States, we have representatives in our government that speak for groups of people. These representatives make sure their constituents, or the people they represent, are treated fairly.

Many representatives serve communities that have large numbers of minorities, and they fight for the rights of these minorities in the government. By listening to what minority groups want, representatives help make sure new laws are as fair as possible to everyone, including minorities.

THE SPIRIT OF DEMOCRACY

Martin Luther King Jr. fought tirelessly for the rights of African Americans. He also fought for the rights of other Americans who were poor and disadvantaged.

Laws in the United States are made by Congress and then signed into law by the president. Citizens vote for both the president and the people who represent them in Congress.

15

WHAT IS FAIR FOR MINORITIES TO EXPECT?

Since the United States is a democracy, new laws likely won't favor minority groups. However, even though they may not get favorable laws or decisions, minorities hopefully won't get laws that discriminate or target them either.

Imagine you're **allergic** to peanuts, and your class is voting on what kind of candy to get for Halloween. You might not get the candy you want, but you can fairly expect that the class won't pick one with peanuts because it means you will be left out.

> Barack Obama was the first African American and minority president of the United States.

WHY ARE MINORITY RIGHTS IMPORTANT?

Minority rights need to be protected. Citizens should be aware of the **tyranny** of the majority. This is when the majority decides all laws. If this happens, minorities may find themselves with no rights, unable to successfully and meaningfully be active members of society.

Minorities have much to offer the majority, including new ideas and different ways of looking at things. Any society where the minority is left out will not be as good as one in which they're accepted and given a voice.

THE SPIRIT OF DEMOCRACY

Ta-Nehisi Coates has written several books and articles about his own **experiences** being a minority in the United States. He offers meaningful suggestions for how our country can change and improve.

Ta-Nehisi Coates is one of the most important voices today when it comes to talking about why minority rights matter.

WHAT SOCIETY IS BEST?

The best society for minorities is one that takes them and their views **seriously**. It's the society that gives all people an equal and fair chance to be active in their communities and government. Minorities won't always get exactly what they want, but they'll never be made to feel targeted or left out of society.

Even now, in the United States, we come up short sometimes. But our democracy is always moving toward being more **inclusive** and fair.

> The society that's best for minorities is one in which their voices are always heard and taken seriously.

20

MINORITY RIGHTS

Minority rights are an important part of any good democracy. Democracy may mean the vote of the majority makes laws, but it also means people won't be hurt or discriminated against because they're in the minority.

People who live in a society where minority rights are protected can live happier lives because they know that if they ever become the minority on an issue, they'll be given those same protections. Minority rights are a key part of a healthy democracy.

GLOSSARY

allergic: Having a bad bodily reaction to certain foods, animals, or surroundings.

discriminate: To treat people unequally based on class, race, or religion.

economic: Having to do with the amount of buying and selling in a place.

ethnicity: Of or relating to large groups of people who have the same customs, religion, and origin.

experience: Skill or knowledge you get by doing something. Also, to do or see something.

gender: Relating to a person being male or female.

inclusive: Open to everyone.

punish: To make someone suffer for wrongdoing.

represent: To act officially for someone or something.

responsibility: Something a person is in charge of.

serious: Dealing with matters in a thoughtful way, not trying to be funny.

target: The focus of an attack.

tyranny: A government in which one ruler has all the power.

INDEX

D
discrimination, 12, 16, 20, 22

E
ethnicity, 6

F
free speech, 8

G
gender, 6, 8

L
laws, 4, 10, 14–16, 18

M
minority groups, 6

P
politics, 6
protection, 10, 12, 18, 22

R
race, 6
religion, 6
representatives, 10-11, 14

T
taxes, 8
tyranny, 18

V
voting, 8, 10-11, 15, 16, 22

WEBSITES

Due to the changing nature of Internet links, PowerKids Press has developed an online list of websites related to the subject of this book. This site is updated regularly. Please use this link to access the list: www.powerkidslinks.com/pofd/min

24